DINOSAURS
DISCOVERED

FIRST EDITION

Editors Katy Lennon, Kritika Gupta, Abhijit Dutta; **Project Art Editors** Emma Hobson, Yamini Panwar;
Art Editor Shubham Rohatgi; **US Editor** Jennette ElNaggar; **US Senior Editor** Shannon Beatty;
Jacket Coordinator Francesca Young; **Jacket Designer** Dheeraj Arora;
DTP Designers Dheeraj Singh, Mohd Rizwan; **Picture Researcher** Sakshi Saluja;
Producer, Pre-Production Dragana Puvacic; **Producer** Barbara Ossawska;
Managing Editors Laura Gilbert, Monica Saigal; **Managing Art Editor** Diane Peyton Jones;
Deputy Managing Art Editor Ivy Sengupta; **Delhi Team Head** Malavika Talukder;
Creative Director Helen Senior; **Publishing Director** Sarah Larter;
Reading Consultant Linda Gambrell, PhD; **Educational Consultant** Jacqueline Harris

THIS EDITION

Editorial Management by Oriel Square
Produced for DK by WonderLab Group LLC
Jennifer Emmett, Erica Green, Kate Hale, *Founders*

Editors Grace Hill Smith, Libby Romero, Michaela Weglinski;
Photography Editors Kelley Miller, Annette Kiesow, Nicole DiMella; **Managing Editor** Rachel Houghton;
Designers Project Design Company; **Researcher** Michelle Harris; **Copy Editor** Lori Merritt;
Indexer Connie Binder; **Proofreader** Larry Shea; **Reading Specialist** Dr. Jennifer Albro;
Curriculum Specialist Elaine Larson

Published in the United States by DK Publishing
1745 Broadway, 20th Floor, New York, NY 10019

Copyright © 2023 Dorling Kindersley Limited
DK, a Division of Penguin Random House LLC
22 23 24 25 26 10 9 8 7 6 5 4 3 2 1
001–333372–May/2023

All rights reserved.

Without limiting the rights under the copyright reserved above, no part of this publication may be reproduced, stored in or introduced into a retrieval system, or transmitted, in any form, or by any means (electronic, mechanical, photocopying, recording, or otherwise), without the prior written permission of the copyright owner.
Published in Great Britain by Dorling Kindersley Limited

A catalog record for this book
is available from the Library of Congress.
HC ISBN: 978-0-7440-6581-7
PB ISBN: 978-0-7440-6582-4

DK books are available at special discounts when purchased in bulk for sales promotions, premiums,
fundraising, or educational use. For details, contact: DK Publishing Special Markets,
1745 Broadway, 20th Floor, New York, NY 10019
SpecialSales@dk.com

Printed and bound in China

The publisher would like to thank the following for their kind permission to reproduce their images:
a=above; c=center; b=below; l=left; r=right; t=top; b/g=background

123RF.com: alexeykonovalenko 6-7bc, leonello calvetti 37tc; **Alamy Stock Photo:** Javier Etcheverry 43, GL Archive 20cl, Stocktrek Images, Inc. / Nobumichi Tamura 22-23b; **Dorling Kindersley:** Andy Crawford / Robert L. Braun 37cra, Andy Crawford / Royal Tyrrell Museum of Palaeontology, Alberta, Canada 8, Andy Crawford Courtesy of Dorset Dinosaur Museum 9b; **Getty Images:** Science Photo Library / Roger Harris 20-21; **Shutterstock.com:** Dew_gdragon 9t

Cover image: *Front:* **Dorling Kindersley:** Jon Hughes bc; **Dreamstime.com:** Mark Turner c; **Shutterstock.com:** Herschel Hoffmeyer

All other images © Dorling Kindersley
For more information see: www.dkimages.com

For the curious
www.dk.com

Level 3

DINOSAURS DISCOVERED

Dean R. Lomax

DK

Contents

- **6** Who Studies Dinosaurs?
- **14** Wonders of Europe
- **22** Digging in Asia
- **30** African Adventures

36 Giants of America
46 Glossary
47 Index
48 Quiz

Who Studies Dinosaurs?

From deserts to mountains, dinosaur bones are found all around the world. Each new dinosaur discovery has its own story to tell about how and where these prehistoric animals lived.

Scientists who study dinosaurs look for their fossils. Fossils are the remains of animals and plants that have been left in rocks. They can be millions of years old and can give us clues about the history of our planet. From fossils, scientists can find out what dinosaurs ate, how big they were, and even what color they were.

coprolites, or fossilized dinosaur poop

A team of scientists called paleontologists at an excavation site

7

For a dinosaur to become a fossil, it must have died in special conditions. Many fossils are created when an animal dies close to (or in) water. It then becomes buried by mud or sand at the bottom of the water. Over time, the soft parts of its body rot away, leaving just the hard parts, such as bones and teeth.

As the skeleton is buried deeper, minerals from the watery mud get into the bones. The mud hardens into rock. The bones harden, too, creating a fossil.

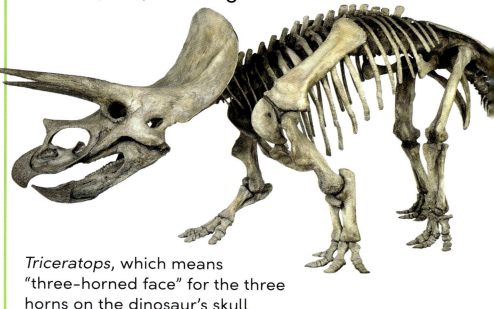

Triceratops, which means "three-horned face" for the three horns on the dinosaur's skull

Naming Dinosaurs

On average, scientists discover a new species of dinosaur every week! When they find a new dinosaur, they get to name it. Dinosaur names are taken from Greek or Latin words. Dinosaurs are often named for a feature, such as sharp teeth or horns. Others are named after the place they were discovered or the person who found them.

fossilized dinosaur skin

Dinosaur Discoveries

Here are some of the most important events in the study of dinosaurs.

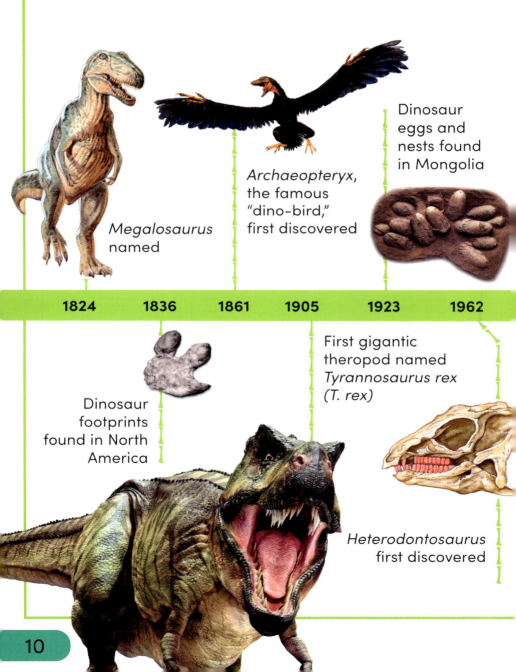

Megalosaurus named

Archaeopteryx, the famous "dino-bird," first discovered

Dinosaur eggs and nests found in Mongolia

1824   **1836**   **1861**   **1905**   **1923**   **1962**

Dinosaur footprints found in North America

First gigantic theropod named *Tyrannosaurus rex* (T. rex)

Heterodontosaurus first discovered

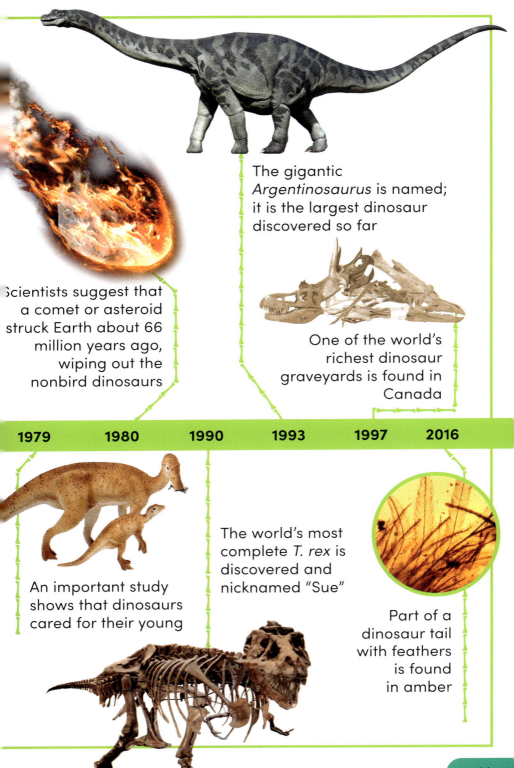

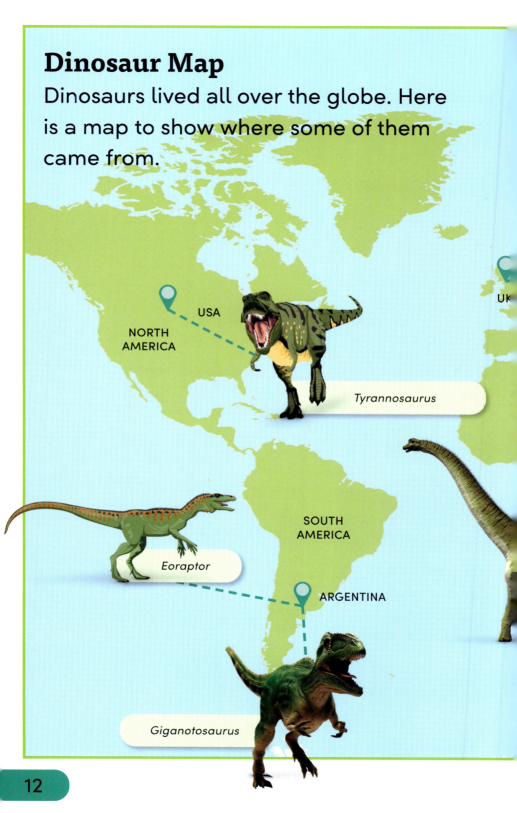

Wonders of Europe

Many early dinosaur discoveries were made in Europe. One of the most important was the "dino-bird," which was found in Germany in 1861. It had a long, bony tail, sharp teeth, and feathers. It was one of the first fossils to show a close link between birds and dinosaurs. Today, scientists place birds and dinosaurs in the same family.

"dino-bird," or *Archaeopteryx*

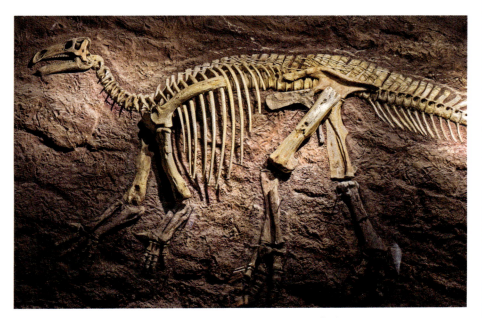

A skeleton of an *Iguanodon*, the type of dinosaur unearthed in Belgium

Nearby, deep inside a Belgian coal mine in 1878, another amazing discovery was made. A herd of more than 30 dinosaur skeletons were found together. It is thought that they all fell down a ravine and drowned when it flooded.

In Portugal many years later, scientists found fossilized dinosaur eggs. The eggs even had unborn babies preserved inside them.

Baryonyx's claw

In 1983, a fossil collector was looking for fossils in a quarry in England. He found an unusual rock, which contained a large claw.

Scientists visited the site and found more than half of the dinosaur's skeleton, including a large skull with teeth in it. It was said to be the find of the century.

The dinosaur lived about 125 million years ago, but its last meal was still preserved in its stomach. It had eaten a tasty meal of fish and other dinosaurs.

Baryonyx walkeri, named after William Walker, the fossil collector who discovered the dinosaur's fossilized claw in a quarry

One dinosaur that lived on an island off the coast of Germany was part of a family of dinosaurs that were the largest dinosaurs to ever walk Earth.

The first bones of this island dinosaur were found in the mid-1990s. Scientists studied them closely. The bones showed a surprise. They were smaller than expected.

These dinosaurs didn't grow as large as those of other dinosaurs in the same family because there wasn't much food for them to eat on their small island.

An *Europasaurus*, a smaller version of its relatives

One group of large dinosaurs, called stegosaurs, had bony plates along their backs and spikes on their tails. The first skeleton in this group to be discovered was found in England in 1874. It had leg bones, armor plates, and tail spines. Its name, *Dacentrurus*, means "very pointy tail."

Discovering Dinosaurs
Famous scientist Sir Richard Owen identified this creature with a pointy tail as a new dinosaur. In fact, Owen was the scientist who coined the word "dinosaur." In 1842, he gave these giant reptiles that once roamed Earth their own name. An expert on animal skeletons, Owen learned that dinosaurs were not just large lizards. They were a separate group of animals.

Stegosaurus

Digging in Asia

The first nonbird dinosaur found with feathers was discovered in China in 1996. This find was more proof that birds and dinosaurs are part of the same family.

One of these dinosaurs was very well preserved. Scientists could even tell what color it was. It was reddish brown and had camouflage patterns and stripes.

The turkey-size *Sinosauropteryx*, the first nonbird dinosaur found with feathers

A *Protoceratops*, the type of dinosaur found buried in the Gobi desert

fossil of a *Sinosauropteryx*

Another exciting dinosaur discovery was made in the Gobi desert. In 1971, scientists dug out fossils of two dinosaurs fighting. The battle had become frozen in time as the pair were buried by sand, possibly from the collapse of a sand dune.

In 2002, scientists visited a desert-like area in China. They found two small skeletons. One of the skeletons belonged to an adult. The other was around 6 years old when it died. The dinosaur was an early ancestor of the *T. rex*. It had a large crest on its head. The crest may have been brightly colored. It could have been used to attract a mate.

Named *Guanlong*, or "crowned dragon," for its head crest

In 1965, a team of scientists found part of a skeleton in the Gobi desert. It had huge arms with powerful claws. Its name means "terrible hand." The missing bones made it difficult for the team to know what the dinosaur looked like.

Deinocheirus claw

The ostrich-like *Deinocheirus*; scientists think its wide toe claws kept it from sinking into muddy riverbanks.

It was thought to have been a giant meat eater that walked on two legs. For almost 50 years, it remained one of the most mysterious dinosaurs ever discovered.

In 2014, the mystery behind the giant claws was solved! Two more skeletons were found. The dinosaur was the largest member of the ostrich-like group of dinosaurs.

Days of the Dinosaurs

Dinosaurs flourished for more than 165 million years. This time was split into three periods. Follow the lines to match the dinosaurs to when they lived.

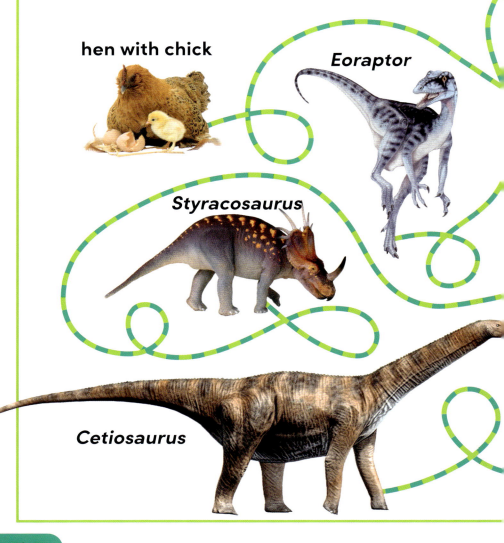

Triassic Period

This period was 252 to 201 million years ago. The first dinosaurs appeared around 231 million years ago.

Jurassic Period

This period was 201 to 145 million years ago. Some of the largest dinosaurs first appeared at this time.

Cretaceous Period

The last of the nonbird dinosaurs died during this period 145 to 66 million years ago.

Today

There are dinosaurs alive today—they are birds!

29

African Adventures

A lot of dinosaur fossils have been collected from all across Africa. In 1976, a cluster of six eggs was found in South Africa. Five eggs still contained unborn babies. The eggs belonged to a plant-eating dinosaur.

Another dinosaur found in Africa could live in and out of water and had large spines on its back. The spines formed a sail or hump. This sail may have been used for display or defense, or to help the dinosaur control its temperature.

An almost complete embryo, or unborn baby, of *Massospondylus*

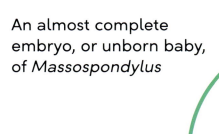

A *Spinosaurus* with its crocodile-like mouth and large sail sticking out of the water

There are many large animals alive today, but none as tall as a dinosaur found in Tanzania.

It was one of the tallest dinosaurs ever and was twice the height of a giraffe. That's why its name means "giant giraffe." And also like giraffes, they used their long necks to eat leaves from the treetops.

It was also one of the heaviest dinosaurs. It weighed about the same as five adult African elephants!

A wandering herd of long-necked *Giraffatitans*

Skeleton of *Heterodontosaurus*

In South Africa, between 1961 and 1962, a team of scientists found a skull, a jaw, and some teeth that belonged to an interesting dinosaur.

It was about the size of a fox. It belonged to a family of dinosaurs that had special teeth. Most dinosaurs had lots of the same type of tooth in their mouths. But these dinosaurs had different kinds of teeth. This suggests that they may have eaten both plants and animals.

This fox-size dinosaur may have had coarse bristles on its skin.

Giants of America

Many dinosaur discoveries in the Americas have helped us understand a lot about how these animals lived. The largest dinosaur and the oldest dinosaur were both found in South America!

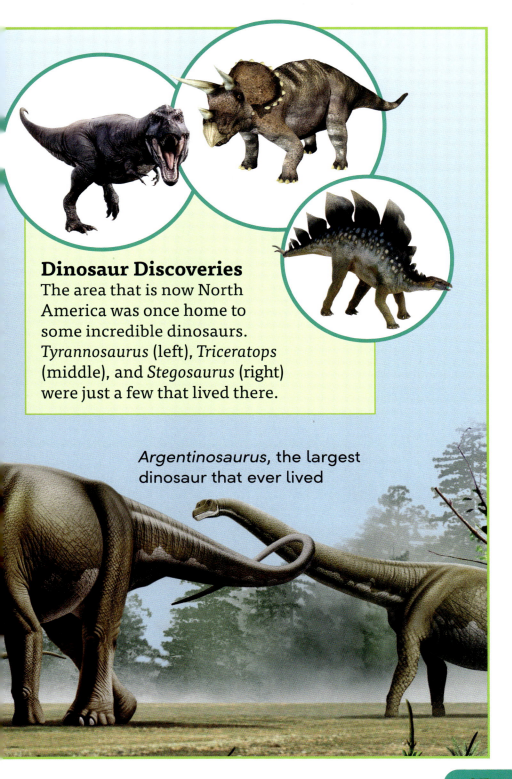

Dinosaur Discoveries

The area that is now North America was once home to some incredible dinosaurs. *Tyrannosaurus* (left), *Triceratops* (middle), and *Stegosaurus* (right) were just a few that lived there.

Argentinosaurus, the largest dinosaur that ever lived

The group of dinosaurs that are often called raptors were fast. They had sharp teeth and claws. Many species were quite small—about the size of a turkey. In 2005, part of a skeleton was found in South Dakota. Ten years later, the bones were identified as a new species. This dinosaur was almost twice as long as a polar bear, making it one of the largest raptor dinosaurs known.

Named *Dakotaraptor* after where its skeleton was found, this dinosaur probably used its feathers to keep warm.

raptor dinosaur claw

It lived at the same time and in the same area as the giant *T. rex*. Bumps were found on the arm bones of the skeleton. These are called quill knobs. They suggest that this dinosaur had feathers.

39

In 2011, news broke that an exciting fossil had been uncovered in Canada. Scientists visited the site. They were amazed to find that the skeleton was an almost complete armored dinosaur.

It is so well preserved that the 110-million-year-old fossil looks as if it is sleeping. Bits of color were even found in its skin. They show that the animal was reddish brown.

Borealopelta, the best-preserved armored dinosaur ever found

Dinosaurs are often found by teams who go looking for them. But many are found by chance and often in unusual situations.

In 1993, a man was riding through the badlands of Patagonia, Argentina. He suddenly saw a giant leg bone sticking out of the sand! A team of scientists rushed there to see what else they could find.

This accidental discovery turned out to be a big find. This new species was large enough to rival the famous *T. rex.* It is the largest meat-eating dinosaur ever found in the southern part of Earth.

Giganotosaurus carolinii, named in honor of Ruben Carolini, who first spotted part of the skeleton in the sand

43

Dinosaurs of Australia and Antarctica

More than 100 million years ago, Australia and Antarctica were joined together. Here are some of the dinosaurs that lived on this ancient land.

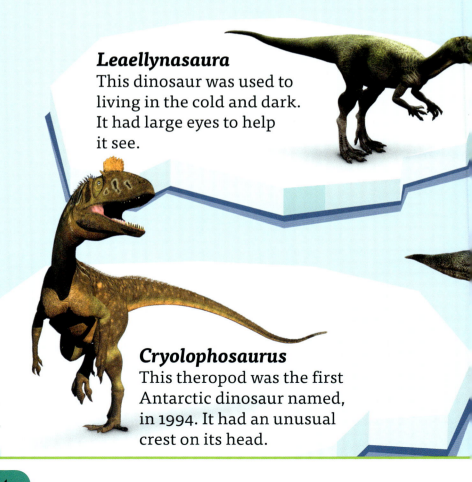

Leaellynasaura
This dinosaur was used to living in the cold and dark. It had large eyes to help it see.

Cryolophosaurus
This theropod was the first Antarctic dinosaur named, in 1994. It had an unusual crest on its head.

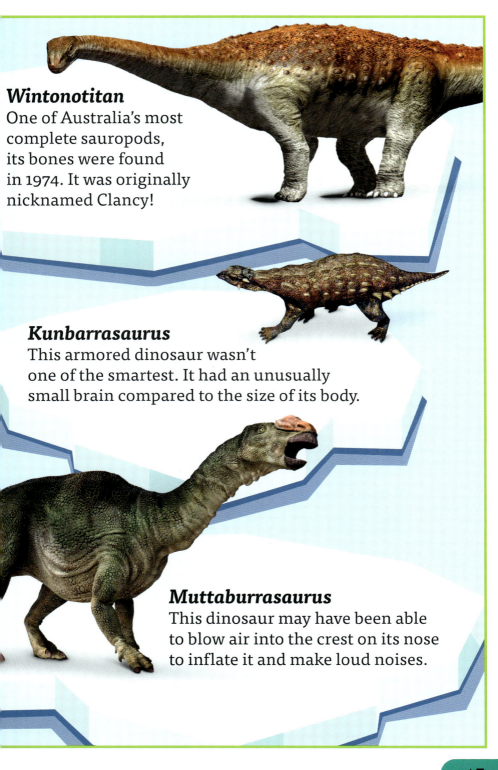

Wintonotitan
One of Australia's most complete sauropods, its bones were found in 1974. It was originally nicknamed Clancy!

Kunbarrasaurus
This armored dinosaur wasn't one of the smartest. It had an unusually small brain compared to the size of its body.

Muttaburrasaurus
This dinosaur may have been able to blow air into the crest on its nose to inflate it and make loud noises.

Glossary

Ancestor
An animal or plant to which a more recent animal or plant is related

Badlands
A vast area of land that is often dry, rocky, and difficult to access

Camouflage
Colors or patterns on an animal's skin, fur, or feathers that help it merge with the environment

Embryo
An unborn or unhatched animal

Fossil
Remains or traces of a once-living animal or plant

Paleontologist
A scientist who studies prehistoric life through the examination of fossils

Prehistoric
An ancient time before recorded history

Quill
A stiff, sharp part of a feather or spine

Ravine
A deep, narrow valley

Sand dune
A hill of sand

Sauropod
A group of dinosaurs with long necks and tails

Theropod
A group of meat-eating dinosaurs that stood on two legs

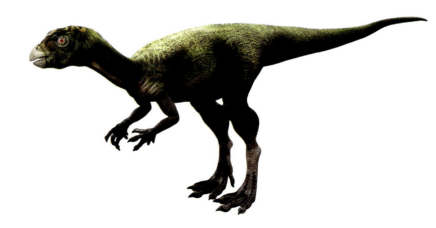

Index

Africa 13, 30–35
Americas 12, 36–43
Antarctica 13, 44–45
Archaeopteryx 10, 14
Argentinosaurus 11, 37
Asia 13, 22–27
Australia 13, 44–45
Baryonyx 16
Baryonyx walkeri 17
birds 14, 22, 29
Borealopelta 40
Carolini, Ruben 42
Cetiosaurus 28
claws 16, 17, 26, 27, 39
color of dinosaurs 22, 40
coprolites 6
crests 24, 25, 44, 45
Cretaceous period 29
Cryolophosaurus 13, 44
Dacentrurus 20
Dakotaraptor 38
Deinocheirus 26-27
"dino-bird" 10, 14
eggs 10, 15, 30
Eoraptor 12, 28
Europasaurus 19
Europe 13, 14–21
feathers 11, 22, 38, 39
footprints 10
fossils 6, 8, 9, 23
Giganotosaurus 12
Giganotosaurus carolinii 42
Giraffatitan 13, 33

Guanlong 25
Heterodontosaurus 10, 34
Iguanodon 15
Jurassic period 29
Kunbarrasaurus 45
Leaellynasaura 13, 44
map 12–13
Massospondylus 31
Megalosaurus 10, 13
Microraptor 13
Muttaburrasaurus 45
naming dinosaurs 9
Owen, Sir Richard 20
paleontologists 7
poop 6
Protoceratops 23
raptors 38, 39
sail 30, 31
sauropods 45
Sinosauropteryx 22, 23
spines 30, 41
Spinosaurus 13, 31
Stegosaurus 21, 37
Styracosaurus 28
time line 10–11
Triassic period 29
Triceratops 8, 37
Tyrannosaurus 12, 37
Tyrannosaurus rex 10, 11, 24, 39
Velociraptor 13
Walker, William 17
Wintonotitan 45

47

Quiz

Answer the questions to see what you have learned. Check your answers in the key below.

1. What is a paleontologist?
2. Which dinosaur was named for the three horns on its skull?
3. Which fossil was one of the first to show a close link between dinosaurs and birds?
4. What does *Deinocheirus* mean?
5. During what period of time did the first dinosaurs appear?
6. True or False: Some dinosaurs had feathers.
7. What makes heterodontosaurs unique among dinosaurs?
8. What is the largest dinosaur on record?

1. A person who studies dinosaurs and prehistoric life
2. *Triceratops* 3. *Archaeopteryx* 4. Terrible hand 5. Triassic period
6. True 7. Different types of teeth 8. *Argentinosaurus*